UNDERSTANDING THE PARANORMAL

INVESTIGATING MAGIC

KATHRYN HORSLEY

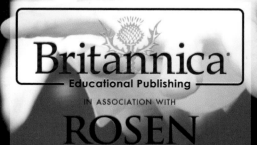

Britannica
Educational Publishing
IN ASSOCIATION WITH
ROSEN
EDUCATIONAL SERVICES

Published in 2017 by Britannica Educational Publishing (a trademark of Encyclopædia Britannica, Inc.) in association with The Rosen Publishing Group, Inc. 29 East 21st Street, New York, NY 10010

Distributed exclusively by Rosen Publishing.
To see additional Britannica Educational Publishing titles, go to rosenpublishing.com.

First Edition

Britannica Educational Publishing
J.E. Luebering: Executive Director, Core Editorial
Anthony L. Green: Editor, Compton's by Britannica

Rosen Publishing
Jacob R. Steinberg: Editor
Nelson Sá: Art Director
Brian Garvey: Designer
Cindy Reiman: Photography Manager
Karen Huang: Photo Researcher

Library of Congress Cataloging-in-Publication Data

Names: Horsley, Kathryn, author.
Title: Investigating magic / Kathryn Horsley.
Description: First Edition. | New York : Britannica Educational Publishing, 2017. | Series: Understanding the paranormal | Includes bibliographical references and index.
Identifiers: LCCN 2015047011| ISBN 9781680485752 (library bound : alk. paper) | ISBN 9781680485813 (pbk. : alk. paper) | ISBN 9781680485585 (6-pack : alk. paper)
Subjects: LCSH: Science and magic—Juvenile literature. | Magic—Social aspects—Juvenile literature.
Classification: LCC BF1623.S35 H67 2016 | DDC 133.4/3—dc23
LC record available at http://lccn.loc.gov/2015047011

Manufactured in the United States of America

CONTENTS

INTRODUCTION

Making the impossible appear possible may not seem like an art, but it truly is. The term "magic" has been applied to a wide range of practices over the ages. Some of these practices are paranormal and involve a true belief in invisible forces. Others serve the purpose of entertainment but nevertheless wow spectators. Magic is a way of thinking that looks to the use of supernatural powers to influence events or cause changes in the material world. Whether magicians truly believe in such powers or simply use sleight of hand to entertain, they challenge an audience's ability to perceive, imagine, and reason.

Practices classified as magic, including religious rituals and entertainment, have been a part of society for a very long time. Throughout history, people have been amazed, perplexed, and even afraid of magic. People who practiced magic have been both praised and persecuted. Over time, people's perception of magic has evolved. Today, magic is perceived as a wondrous act. Successful and skillful magicians are glorified with fame instead of persecution. Magic is becoming increasingly popular and widely accepted in both entertainment and religion. With so much to discover about the art of magic, let the exploration begin (before it vanishes into thin air)!

In The Conjurer, *c. 1502, oil on wood, Dutch painter Hieronymus Bosch illustrates the shell game, a magic trick that utilizes sleight of hand to astound an audience.*

WHAT IS MAGIC?

Magic is a term that refers to many different concepts. It may be used for paranormal practices that believers claim make use of invisible forces. However, in popular culture it also refers to acts of conjuring and sleight of hand for entertainment. In all of its forms, magic offers alternative modes of rationality that challenge how people understand the world around them.

TYPES OF MAGIC

The type of magic that is also sometimes called conjuring can be described as entertainment. It has its roots in other practices called "magic" throughout the ages. These older forms of magic involve aspects of divination, astrology, incantations, alchemy, and sorcery. Spells

By the 18th century magic as entertainment was well established in Europe. In A Street Magician near the Place de la Bastille, Paris, *engraved by H. Jannin, c. 1840–50, a street magician entertains crowds in Paris.*

and incantations are often considered the most important part of a magical rite. They are used to draw power from supernatural elements. Commonly, people associate witchcraft with spells in the form of curses. However, phrases and words that are used to dazzle and misdirect audiences during performances are very important to entertaining magicians as well. Modern magicians use the remnants of a spell for healing when they utter the word "abracadabra" during performances.

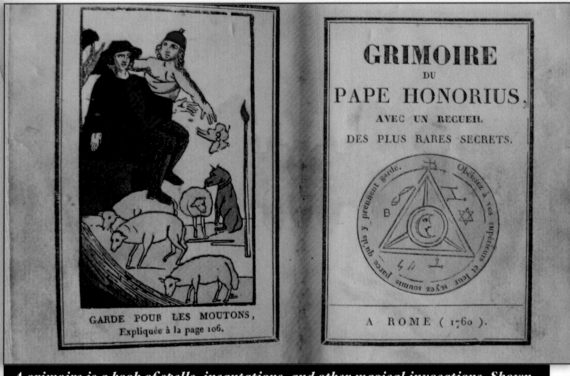

A grimoire is a book of spells, incantations, and other magical invocations. Shown here is the title page of the popular 18th-century grimoire Le Grimoire du Pape Honorius, *claimed to be written by Pope Honorius III.*

Spells and incantations may involve words or symbols. They can be used to draw power from spiritual agencies, nature, or share power within a group. Some spells require the use of herbs, animal parts, or specific gemstones. Spells, incantations, and other phrases are important aspects of the ritualism of magic. Whether for spiritual connection or entertainment value, routines and rituals play a significant role in the effectiveness of magic. Magicians must be able to successfully and consistently manipulate materials or the audience to perform an illusion.

Many people believe in the transformative power of words. Shamans and mediums, for example, repeat

WICCA AND WITCHCRAFT

The terms "Wicca" and "witchcraft" are often used interchangeably and can be confused easily. The main difference is the application of each. Witchcraft is the practice of magic (sometimes for negative or harmful purposes). Wicca is a religion. Wicca is based on elements of traditional witchcraft. It involves the praise of a god, associated with a horned male figure, and a goddess, associated with the Moon. Witchcraft, in turn, does not have a specific deity. Its practitioners do not necessarily believe in an organized religion. Some witches are also Wiccan, but many are not.

When Wicca was created by English author Gerald Gardner in the 1950s, it drew on old pagan beliefs and magical practices. In Wicca, magic is seen as absolute and natural; it is used to grow spiritually or create well-being. The Wicca religion is opposed to doing harm to others.

Gerald Gardner, shown here in a detail from an esoteric triptych, is known for being the founder of Wicca.

Wicca spread widely in the mid-to-late 20th century. Nonetheless, many self-purported witches practice magic outside of the Wicca religion.

specific sounds to achieve an ecstatic state. Other religions use special prayers or psalms to feel closer to spirits.

THE ART OF MAGIC

Performing magic is more than just parlor tricks. It is a skillful delivery of misdirection and dexterity. Magicians must practice their acts thoroughly before going before an audience. Hand-eye coordination is a vastly important skill to master as a magician. A common trick that magicians use to amaze audiences is making something seem to appear out of thin air. Pulling rabbits out of hats or a coin from behind an ear can take years of practice. This is why most magicians tend to specialize with the sort of tricks or illusions they perform based on their abilities.

Magicians use tricks and illusions to give the appearance that they can defy the laws of science but they do not accomplish this without help. Many magicians rely on props to assist them in impressing an audience. Props may contain hidden mirrors, secret compartments, or other equipment the magician can use discreetly.

Levitation, mind-reading, and making things disappear are all illusions that give the impression that the magician can defy the laws of science. One mesmerizing trick performed by David Copperfield, a well-known

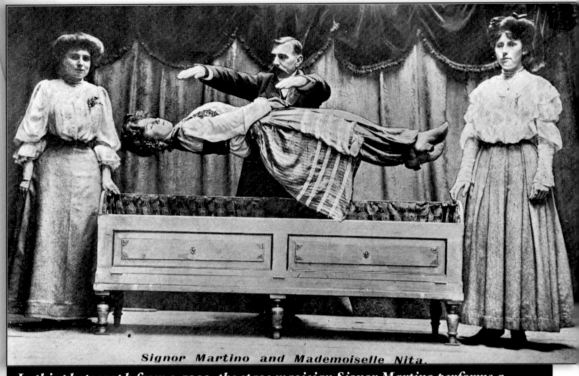

Signor Martino and Mademoiselle Nita.

In this photograph from c. 1900, the stage magician Signor Martino performs a levitating act. This illusion gives the appearance that the magician is capable of defying gravity.

illusionist, was making the Statue of Liberty disappear. The Statue of Liberty was hidden from the audience's view with the help of well-placed lighting and a rotating platform.

GOOD OR EVIL?

Magic can be separated into categories based on its purpose and who is performing it. White magic is used for healing, promoting happiness, or providing protection.

Black magic is the type of magic more often portrayed in television and movies. It is used for destructive purposes. Black magic is considered to be stronger than white magic, and it includes curses or hexes meant to harm another person. Once cursed by black magic, it is said that white magic cannot protect the cursed person. Stage magic, or conjuring used for entertainment, is generally accepted to be harmless.

VOODOO IN HAITI

In Haiti there is a popular religion known as voodoo. As a religion, voodoo has its origins in the African religion of vodun. African slaves brought to Haiti mixed their belief in many spirits with the Roman Catholic belief in a single God (taught to them by French slave owners). The result was voodoo.

Outside of Haiti, voodoo is often associated with legends of black magic. It is generally portrayed by the media as a dark form of magic used by cults or devil worshipers. There are many popular stories about voodoo, including the claim that voodoo leaders can use magic to raise the dead. True Haitian voodoo, however, is most often used to help and heal others instead of for harm or for personal gain.

At a voodoo market in Lomé, Togo, herbs, animal ingredients, and small statues (such as the ones shown here) are sold to magically heal or protect practitioners.

People in Haiti that continue to practice voodoo are sometimes asked to cure the sick, perform rituals for the spirit gods, or repel hexes. Some rituals involve the ritual use of herbs and spells, much like magic.

According to believers, both forms of magic can be performed by the intellectually elite and commoners. When magic is performed using forms of astrology or alchemy, it is considered to be high magic since the performer must be educated in those studies to apply magic to them. Simpler magic, such as the use of charms or sorcery, requires less study and therefore can be practiced by commoners. It is known as low magic.

People have used, accepted, feared, and forbidden magic for ages. With so many applications and such an extensive reach, magic certainly has an undeniable power (even if it is only cultural).

THE HISTORY OF MAGIC

People have believed in magic since ancient times. Descriptions of magical demonstrations were recorded in Egypt as early as 2500 BCE. Such accounts reflect an inevitable mix of fact and fantasy, a quality they share with even their most modern counterparts. Whether used for paranormal purposes or simple entertainment, magic has always evoked captivation, astonishment, and, at times, fear.

ORIGINS OF MAGIC

Throughout history, magical rites have been a part of various cultures and religions. Greeks and Romans believed that magicians had secret knowledge and the ability to channel power through invisible forces. In fact, many of the traditions associated with magic in the Classical world

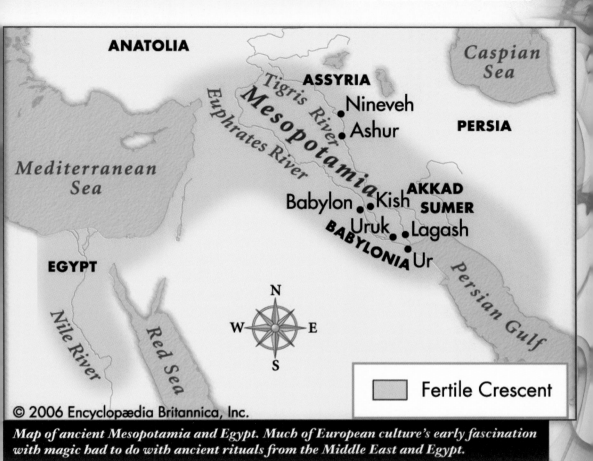

Map of ancient Mesopotamia and Egypt. Much of European culture's early fascination with magic had to do with ancient rituals from the Middle East and Egypt.

came from a fascination with ancient Middle Eastern beliefs and are concerned with a need for countermagic against sorcery. Countermagic is a type of magic used to provide protection against black magic or sorcerers with harmful intentions. The use of spells as countermagic is first recorded in ancient Mesopotamia and Egypt.

In ancient Italy, the Etruscan people read the entrails, or bowels, of animal sacrifices to predict the future. This method of prediction is called haruspicy.

An engraving by Jacques Grasset de Saint-Sauveur published in L'Antique Rome *(1796) illustrates the practice of haruspicy, in which the bowels of an animal sacrifice were interpreted to predict the future.*

Oomancy was another practice that used an egg for divination. In oomancy an egg is cracked open into water, and the shapes it makes are interpreted.

In ancient Rome, the behavior of birds was closely monitored as a means of predicting the future. This practice is called augury. Originally augury was performed by magistrates, and it played a role in political decision-making. The Romans sometimes used augury to determine whether or not they had the gods' approval before going into battle.

Many cultures used magic as a helpful source of knowledge. Magic was not outlawed. Instead, it had important uses. However, with time the perception of magic and those who practice it would change.

A TURN FOR THE DARK SIDE

In early Christian Europe magic came to be identified with paganism, the negative term Christians used to refer to Celtic, Germanic, and Scandinavian

In the Middle Ages, magic came to be associated with paganism and witchcraft. In this engraving from the Compendium Maleficarum *(1626) by Francesco Maria Guazzo, the devil makes his victims trample on a cross.*

religious beliefs. Nevertheless, Christians often used magic, particularly countermagic, during this time period. For example, some medicinal remedies found in monks' manuscripts combined Christian formulas and rites with Germanic folk rituals. These remedies were intended to cure ailments caused by black magic, poisons, or demonic possession.

By the Middle Ages magic became associated with devil worship. It was thought that magicians got their

MALLEUS MALEFICARUM

The *Malleus maleficarum* was a detailed handbook used to identify and fight witchcraft. The manual was written in about 1486 by Heinrich Kramer and Jacob Sprenger. Both men were members of the Dominican Order of monks. Its name, *Malleus maleficarum*, is Latin for "Hammer of Witches."

The *Malleus* identified witchcraft as a dangerous practice associated with the devil. It outlined how to identify, question, convict, and kill witches. Soon after the *Malleus* was published, the printing press was invented. This led to the manual's wide distribution. Its influence lasted well into the 18th century, and it inspired two centuries of witch-hunting in Europe.

powers by making deals with the devil. Magicians were often caught up in condemnations of witches, sorcerers, and devil worshipers. They were often jailed and sometimes executed. Nevertheless, many spell books and other manuals of magic were still published during this time. Royals and nobles continued to be interested in the uses of magic.

Despite persecution of so-called black magic, forms of what was known as "white magic" remained popular.

The Swiss physician and chemist Paracelsus, illustrated here in a copy of his Astronomica et Astrologica Pouscula (1567), mixed magic and other occult traditions to create medical treatments and cures.

This magic blended magic, mysticism, and other occult traditions. During the Renaissance, there was renewed interest in ancient Middle Eastern practices, Neoplatonic mysticism, and Arabic texts on alchemy and astrology. Such magical practices were tolerated, as they were believed to be part of the Jewish and Christian Hermetic traditions.

MAGIC AND THE MODERN WORLD

Europeans' concepts about magic, religion, and science were brought to other parts of the world in the modern period by traders, conquerors, missionaries, anthropologists, and historians. European travelers in the 16th–19th centuries took a primitive approach to studying non-European cultures. Their accounts were influenced by Christian beliefs about religion. Spiritual practices of colonialized peoples were considered magic, rather than religions. In the Europeans' mind, this justified colonizing and converting other peoples. In the late 19th century, anthropologists began to study magic and its part in different world religions.

Today, a popular "scientific" worldview in Western societies suggests the triumph of human reason. The Enlightenment and the scientific revolution celebrated

MAGIC AS ENTERTAINMENT

As a result of the persecution of magicians, texts began to be widely published explaining the illusions of conjurers and the scientific principles behind many magic tricks. At this time, a distinction was more firmly drawn between black magic and magic as entertainment. While black magic was outlawed, traveling entertainers, such as jugglers and other "wonder workers," could continue to perform before royalty, nobility, and even bishops—if not always for the public. By the 16th century professional magicians were doing card tricks, reading minds, and making objects disappear. Public performances of magic took place outdoors at carnivals, fairs, and markets. By the 18th century magic as entertainment was well established in Europe.

Most of the British Colonies of North America were under the influence of the Puritans, a Christian group that frowned on "idle amusements" as works of the devil. Magicians were outlawed in some colonies. However, by the time of the American Revolution, public attitudes toward magicians had become more tolerant. Several European magicians made their way to the United States after 1776. In the 18th and 19th centuries, magic gradually became more associated with stage performance than with witchcraft.

In modern times, magic persists in stage entertainment. Shown here is the popular stage magician Harry Blackstone, Jr., entertaining an audience by "sawing" his assistant in half during a performance on March 5, 1975.

scientific reasoning over magic. This is evident, for example, in 19th-century exposés of magic tricksters as frauds. Modern popular magic has been relegated to the realm of entertainment. It often appears as a plot device in stories and movies, as tricks aimed at children, and as mysterious sleight-of-hand illusions in magic shows that delight the audience's sense perceptions and challenge their reasoning ability.

Meanwhile, the magical rites associated with various world religions have slowly gained wider acceptance. In the Western world, the occult survives in popular interests like astrology and New Age religion. Magic, in a stricter sense, thrives in the Wicca religion.

In the United States, courts have upheld practitioners' rights to perform magical rituals. In *Dettmer v. Landon* (1986), a court defended the standing of Wicca as a legitimate religion. In *Church of Lukumi Babalu Aye v. City of Hialeah* (1993), the Supreme Court ruled that animal sacrifices, when performed as a religious ceremony, were legal. Furthermore, the late 20th and early 21st centuries saw a continued academic interest in magical practices worldwide. Anthropologists have studied the magical rites of nonurban cultures with great interest.

CHAPTER THREE

THE MECHANICS OF "MAGIC" AND ITS LEGENDARY PRACTITIONERS

Although magic today is largely confined to the entertainment industry, its goal is still to give the impression that people can do the impossible. Audiences are awed by seemingly supernatural feats. However, there are many plausible explanations for the spectacular feats performed by highly skilled magicians. Let's debunk some of magic's most convincing tricks.

PULLING RABBITS OUT OF HATS

One of the most iconic stage magicians of all time was French magician Jean-Eugène Robert-Houdin (1805–71), "the father of modern magic." Interested in science, he was the first magician to use electro-magnetism in his act. He also denounced magicians who claimed psychic powers or other supernatural help for their tricks.

Jean-Eugène Robert-Houdin (1805–71) is widely accepted as the "father of modern magic" and specialized in grand illusions.

One of Robert-Houdin's most famous tricks involved production—making an object appear out of nowhere. In one impressive act, Robert-Houdin seemingly made a

27

handkerchief disappear while standing near a barren orange tree. The handkerchief then reappeared inside an orange that he commanded to grow on the tree. This illusion bedazzled audiences. In reality, Robert-Houdin made the oranges "suddenly" bloom with the help of a key, which he used to trigger gears and other mechanisms within the base of the tree. A previously prepared orange already had a handkerchief within and voilà!

John Henry Anderson (1814–74) was a Scottish conjurer who performed throughout Europe and the United States in the mid-19th century. Anderson is best remembered as the magician who pulled a rabbit from a seemingly empty hat. He didn't originate the trick, but he did

John Henry Anderson (1814–74) made both pulling a rabbit out of a hat and catching a bullet with his teeth popular tricks for rival magicians to emulate.

make it popular. The hat trick is performed by placing the empty hat on a surface with a hidden opening. The rabbit (or sometimes a bouquet of flowers) is then raised into the hat by an assistant before the big reveal.

VANISHING INTO THIN AIR

The opposite of production is disappearance. One master of this technique was Harry Blackstone, Sr. (1885–1965). Blackstone was an American magician who performed in vaudeville and toured widely. One of his most famous tricks was the "vanishing birdcage." He would cause a rectangular birdcage to seemingly disappear

Harry Blackstone, Sr. (1885–1965) was a popular American magician who specialized in making objects disappear onstage, among other tricks. He was best known for his "vanishing birdcage" illusion.

into thin air. In truth, Blackstone's birdcage was collapsible. The moment he no longer supported the cage, it flattened, and Blackstone pulled it up his sleeve via an elastic cord. In another illusion, Blackstone made a horse disappear.

One of the most famous illusionists to make large objects disappear is American magician David Copperfield

DISTRACTING THE MIND

Robert-Houdin once stated: "To succeed as a conjurer, three things are essential—first, dexterity; second, dexterity; and third, dexterity." Successfully performing an illusion requires practice and skill. Today, most audiences do not believe in magic as a supernatural force. Therefore, magicians must be masters of the art of distraction. Distracting the audience allows the magician to perform a trick without the audience uncovering how it's completed. Some distraction techniques include hand-eye coordination, sleight of hand, hidden mirrors, and secret compartments. Distraction of the mind can be just as useful to a magician as distraction of the eye. Magicians use conversation to misdirect, causing the audience to focus on things other than how the trick is performed.

(1956–). Some of Copperfield's most famous illusions include the disappearance of a Learjet and of the Statue of Liberty in front of a live audience. Making the Statue of Liberty vanish was one of the biggest illusions ever performed and helped make Copperfield famous worldwide.

American magician David Copperfield (1956–) gained fame by performing grand-scaled illusions on live television, which helped make him a widely successful entertainer and a household name.

EXPLAINING OTHER ILLUSIONS

Some magicians give the impression that they can read minds. These magicians are called mentalists. One way to appear to read minds is to utilize silent or verbal signals with the use of an assistant or by reading someone's body language. Robert Heller (1826–78) was a famous English mentalist who began his career in 1869. In his mind-reading act, his assistant was blindfolded and asked a series of questions. Unbeknownst to the audience, the blindfolded assistant was receiving Heller's answers through electrical signals, which the assistant could then interpret. The performance left audiences and even other magicians mystified.

Other acts of magic involve defying the laws of physics. Levitation is the act of causing something to float, rise, or hover in the air without physical means. Many magicians have wowed audiences by making large objects float. Some magicians accomplish this using hydraulics or optical illusions. In one act, American magician Harry Kellar (1849–1922) would raise a sleeping woman's body into mid-air. Kellar's stunt involved a wooden board inside the woman's dress, which was attached to a long metal bar. The bar extended off-stage, where a machine

HARRY HOUDINI

The most famous magician of all time is Harry Houdini. Born in Hungary in 1874, Harry Houdini's real name was Erik Weisz. When he moved to America, he changed his name to Houdini because of his admiration for Jean-Eugène Robert-Houdin. As an illusionist and master magician, Harry Houdini escaped straightjackets, handcuffs, and chains. He was a master showman and knew how to promote his act. Even during World War I, Houdini was able to draw audiences to his performances.

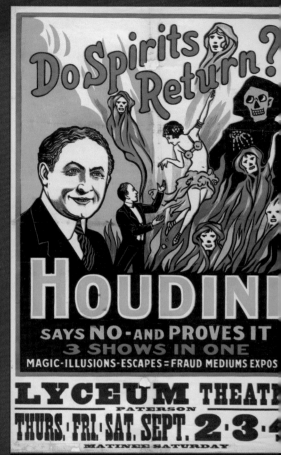

Perhaps the best-known magician of all time, Harry Houdini originated impressive escape routines. He also used his knowledge of sleight of hand to discredit spiritualists.

Harry Houdini began debunking spiritualists after a failed attempt to contact his deceased mother through a medium. His knowledge of sleight of hand helped him uncover tricks that spiritualists used on vulnerable clients. Despite his exposing of fraudulent spiritualists, he and his wife agreed to conduct an experiment in spiritualism: the first to die was to try to communicate with the survivor. His widow declared the experiment a failure before her death in 1943.

Harry Houdini made his fame by performing death-defying stunts. Houdini died on Halloween in 1926 in Detroit, Michigan, after his appendix ruptured.

raised and lowered it. To "prove" she was floating, Kellar would run a hoop back and forth over his assistant's body.

Another iconic illusion was mastered by English magician P.T. Selbit (c. 1879–1938). Selbit is best known for his trick of seemingly sawing a woman in half. In this trick, an assistant is secured in a closed box with her hands and feet tied at opposite ends. The magician then runs a saw through the middle of the box, seemingly cutting the woman in half. In reality, the assistant would slip her feet loose and contain herself in one half of the box before Selbit ran his saw down the middle.

MAGIC'S PLACE IN POPULAR CULTURE

As magic has morphed from supernatural sorcery and spells to a beloved form of stage entertainment, it's also become a part of mainstream popular culture. Notably, magic in fiction is often blended with other paranormal traditions, especially witchcraft. Novels or films about wizards and witches often feature spells, curses, and other forms of magic.

MAGIC IN LITERATURE

Magic has been an important plot element in works of fiction since antiquity. Take into account such episodes from Greek tradition as Odysseus's visit to the island of

This 1923 print depicts the legendary Merlin (right) and King Arthur (left) in Camelot before the Knights of the Round Table. Merlin was said to have used his magical powers to help Arthur gain power and defeat his enemies.

Circe in Homer's *The Odyssey*. An enchantress, Circe cast a spell on Odysseus' men, changing them into pigs. Odysseus himself was protected by an herb given to him by Hermes, messenger of the gods. When Circe realized that Odysseus had been protected, she changed the pigs back into men. *The Golden Ass*, a narrative poem by Roman philosopher Lucius Apuleius (c. 124–170), narrates the adventures of a young man changed by magic into an ass.

In later legends, too, magic played a central role. In the British body of stories about legendary King Arthur, magic features prominently. The prophet and magician Merlin gains his magical powers from a demon but uses them for good causes. It is through Merlin's magic that Arthur rises to power. The tale of Merlin and Arthur was adapted in Disney's *The Sword in the Stone* (1963).

Magic also appears in works written during the Renaissance. Perhaps the best-known example is the hero of William Shakespeare's *The Tempest* (1623), the sorcerer Prospero. The rightful duke of Milan, Prospero is set to sea by his brother, who steals his title. After becoming shipwrecked on an enchanted island, Prospero learns magic and uses it to ultimately regain his throne.

Magic is also popular in children's literature. Most famously, British author J.K. Rowling (1965–) has captured the imagination of children and adults alike with her best-selling series of books about Harry Potter, a young sorcerer in training. The books were critically acclaimed

British actor Daniel Radcliffe, shown here, played the wizard Harry Potter in the film adaptations of author J. K. Rowling's wildly successful children's novels.

as well as wildly popular and were credited with generating a new interest in reading among children. Filled with fantasy and wonderment, the series centers around Hogwarts School of Witchcraft and Wizardry, where young wizards and witches study magic and related subjects. The series spawned a movie franchise, action figures, memorabilia, and games.

MAGICAL GAMES

Sorcerers and witches have made their appearance in a variety of game formats as well. In 1991, Nintendo released the video game *The Magician*, which centered around an apprentice magician, Paul, on a quest to defeat the evil sorcerer Abadon. Paul can combine sounds to create more powerful spells as he attempts to rid the land of evil beasts and make his way to Abadon's castle. *Magicka* (2011) was a highly successful video game that followed the same premise.

The 1993 video game *Mage: The Ascension* combined various elements of magic, sorcery, witchcraft, and other paranormal traditions to create a world in which all players can change reality by learning magic. Characters aware of their magical abilities are called Magi.

In addition to video games, magic has featured prominently in card games. First released in 1993, the trading card game *Magic: The Gathering* turns each player into a wizard. Each card represents a spell, magical object, or mythical creature that the player may use in battle to defeat his or her opponent.

Magic: The Gathering *is a popular trading card game that features a deck of over 60 cards representing spells and other magical objects or creatures.*

Lev Grossman's 2009 novel *The Magicians* tells a similar tale of a Brooklyn, N.Y., high school student who is accepted to attend a college for magic. Grossman completed his series with two more books: *The Magician King* (2011) and *The Magician's Land* (2014).

MAGIC IN FILM AND TELEVISION

In Hollywood, magic has also made a strong showing. Tod Browning (1880–1962), the American director who specialized in films about the grotesque, directed *West of Zanzibar* (1928). Based on the 1926 Broadway play *Kongo*, *West of Zanzibar* tells the tale of "Dead-Legs" Phroso, a paralyzed

Dr. Albert Emanuel Vogler, played by actor Max von Sydow, leads a group of traveling performers to a town whose inhabitants try to disprove their magical feats in Ingmar Bergman's The Magician (1958).

former magician who raises his rival's daughter without knowing that she is actually his own.

In 1958 Swedish director Ingmar Bergman (1918–2007) directed *The Magician* (1958). In it, one town's authorities try to stop traveling magician Dr. Albert Emanuel Vogler's show after they hear reports of supernatural occurrences at his previous performance. The film specifically addresses the tension between scientific rationalism and the illusion of show magic.

The Illusionist (2006) makes reference to famous stage magic performed by Jean-Eugène Robert-Houdin. In it, a magician attempts to use his illusions to make a woman fall in love with him after she volunteers to assist during one of his shows. In *The Prestige* (2006), two magicians attempt to sabotage and reveal the secrets behind each other's tricks. In *Now You See Me* (2013), four independent magicians come together under the orders of a magician's secret society called "The Eye." The group works on an elaborate plan to rob a bank during a magic performance and then give the money to the audience.

Magic hasn't just been limited to the big screen. Many television shows have used magic as a major plot element. The third season of the popular series *American Horror Story,* subtitled *Coven,* followed a group of teenage witches who perfected their magical skills. Set in New Orleans, the show blended various paranormal

THE MAGIC CASTLE

The Magic Castle in Los Angeles, California, is a premier venue and restaurant as well as a private club for today's magicians. Founded in 1909, the Magic Castle is comprised of close to 2,500 members. All members must audition before a reviewing committee, which helps maintain the club's elite status among magicians.

The Magic Castle also works to improve the skills of future magicians with its Junior Group. Junior Group members, who are ages 13 to 20, experience one-of- a-kind workshops and lectures from some of the biggest names in magic. They even perform during an annual Future Stars of Magic show. Like all members of the Magic Castle, members of the Junior Group must be highly talented and audition for membership.

Actors Taissa Farmiga, Jamie Brewer, and Emma Roberts appear here in their roles as young witches on American Horror Story: Coven. *Each of the show's seasons blends magic and other occult traditions in otherwise realistic settings.*

traditions, including popular culture's take on Louisiana voodoo.

Whether in movies, books, or real life, magic brings mystery and delight to audiences. For believers, magic accesses important invisible forces to achieve the unthinkable. Even non-believers can be wowed by the art of stage magic, which makes the impossible seem easy. While magic was not always widely accepted or understood, it's been a part of many cultures and religions throughout history. Today magicians can practice their skills and talents without fear of harm. And we can appreciate the history of magic and its place in our culture like never before.

GLOSSARY

ALCHEMY A medieval chemical science with the goals of changing less valuable metals into gold, discovering a single cure for all diseases, and discovering how to live forever.

ASTROLOGY The study of the supposed influences of the stars on human affairs by their positions in relation to each other.

CONJURE To produce as if by magic.

DEXTERITY Ease and grace in physical activity; skill and ease in using the hands.

DIVINATION The art or practice of using omens or magic powers to foretell the future.

ESOTERIC Taught to or understood by members of a special group.

HERMETIC Of or relating to the mystical and alchemical writings or teachings arising in the first three centuries CE and attributed to Hermes Trismegistus.

HYDRAULICS A science that deals with uses of liquid (as water) in motion.

ILLUSION A misleading image presented to the vision; something that deceives or misleads intellectually.

INCANTATION A series of words used to produce a magic spell.

MYSTICISM The belief that direct knowledge of God, spiritual truth, or ultimate reality can be attained through subjective experience (as intuition or insight).

NEOPLATONISM Platonism (the philosophy of Plato) modified in later antiquity to accord with Aristotelian, post-Aristotelian, and eastern conceptions that conceives of the world as an emanation from an ultimate indivisible being with whom the soul is capable of being reunited in trance or ecstasy.

OCCULT Of or relating to supernatural powers or practices.

SABOTAGE To destroy or block the actions of another.

SORCERY The use of powers gotten with the help of or by the control of evil spirits.

SPIRITUALISM A belief that the spirits of the dead communicate with the living.

TRIPTYCH A picture (such as a painting) that has three panels placed next to each other.

FOR FURTHER READING

Alexander, Audrey. *Witches and Wicca* (Supernatural). Pittsburgh, PA: Eldorado Ink, 2015.

Cooke, Tim. *Magic and Illusions* (Mystery Files). New York, NY: Crabtree Publishing Company, 2015.

Ellis, Carol. *New Orleans Voodoo* (Supernatural). Pittsburgh, PA: Eldorado Ink, 2015.

Gross, Peter, and Walter Foster Jr. Creative Team. *101 Ways to Amaze & Entertain: Amazing Magic & Hilarious Jokes to Try on Your Friends & Family*. Orange County, CA: Walter Foster Jr. Publishing, 2015.

Hansen, Grace. *Harry Houdini: Illusionist & Stunt Performer*. Minneapolis, MN: ABDO Kids, 2016.

Jarrow, Gail. *The Amazing Harry Kellar: Great American Magician*. Honesdale, PA: Calkins Creek, 2012.

Jay, Joshua. *Big Magic for Little Hands*. New York, NY: Workman Publishing Company, 2014.

Martineau, Susan. *Marvelous Magic* (Awesome Activities). New York, NY: Windmill Books, 2012.

Mills, J. Elizabeth. *Witches in America* (America's Supernatural Secrets). New York, NY: Rosen Publishing Group, 2012.

Netzley, Patricia D. *Do Witches Exist?* (Do They Exist?). San Diego, CA: ReferencePoint Press, 2016.

Shea, Theresa. *Investigating Witches and Witchcraft* (Understanding the Paranormal). New York, NY: Britannica Educational Publishing, 2015.

Turnbull, Stephanie. *Magic Skills*. Mankato, MN: Smart Apple Media, 2013.

WEBSITES

Because of the changing nature of Internet links, Rosen Publishing has developed an online list of websites related to the subject of this book. This site is updated regularly. Please use this link to access this list:

http://www.rosenlinks.com/UTP/magic

INDEX